C000055934

TO 🐾

FROM 🐾

DATE 🐾

Cat Laughs

Illustrations by
Gary Patterson

HARVEST HOUSE PUBLISHERS
EUGENE, OREGON

Cat Laughs

Text Copyright © 2010 by Harvest House Publishers
Artwork Copyright © 2010 by Gary Patterson

Published by Harvest House Publishers
Eugene, Oregon 97402
www.harvesthousepublishers.com

ISBN 978-0-7369-2657-7

Original illustrations by Gary Patterson, all rights reserved

Design and production by Koechel Peterson & Associates, Inc., Minneapolis, Minnesota

Harvest House Publishers has made every effort to trace the ownership of all poems and quotes. In the event of a question arising from the use of a poem or quote, we regret any error made and will be pleased to make the necessary correction in future editions of this book.

Printed in China

10 11 12 13 14 15 16 / LP / 10 9 8 7 6 5 4 3 2 1

Dedicated to all the pet lovers
owned by their cats.

{ Gary Patterson }

Imp (short for Impulse)
had a favorite early-morning
game she loved to play.
When outside, she would climb a pole
next to my mobile home and get onto
the roof. Then she would noisily run
up and down the length of the house until
I stepped out the back door and held
a laundry basket above my head. That was
her cue to jump into "the elevator" and come
inside for breakfast. If the neighbors ever
noticed me in my nighttime attire
holding a laundry basket out the
back door while calling, "Jump!"
they never mentioned it.

Peg R.

TOP TEN

Things Cats Do While Their Parents Are Away

- Hide marbles, pens, and paper clips in shoes
- Change the time on every clock by 3 minutes
- Play "Cat Scratch Fever" on Guitar Hero over and over
- Post family valuables on eBay
- Post the dog on eBay
- Invite cats off the street to use the litter box
- Invite friends over for a mean game of Go Fish
- Plant evidence of marbles, pens, and paper clips near the dog's bed
- Make crank calls to Animal Control
- Use the dog whistle to play "The Song That Never Ends"

My large tuxedo cat, **Merlin**, meets me by my garage every night. If I tarry too long at my mailbox before walking down my long drive, he runs to meet me. *As* soon as I head down the driveway, Merlin turns around and saunters down the *middle* of the road, tail held high, allowing me to follow him home…at about a sixteenth of a mile per hour.

LaVonne J.

Of all God's creatures, there is only one that cannot be made the slave of the lash. That one is the cat. If man could be crossed with a cat it would improve man, but it would deteriorate the cat.

MARK TWAIN

"Was there ever a time when they didn't catch mice?" your Aunt Amy asked, surprised for the third time.

"Oh, yes indeed," Mrs. Mouser said in a matter-of-fact tone. "All cats used to be good friends with the mice, once upon a time, and it happened that because an old Mrs. Pussy, who lived in the city, didn't have anything in the house to eat, the cats took up catching mice. You see it was in this way: A cat that had always lived in the country made up her mind one day to go and see her cousin in the city, so she put on her bonnet and shawl, wrapped some fried fish in a paper, and started.

"When she got there, her cousin saw the fish, and it made her ashamed because she hadn't anything in the house to offer the visitor, so she asked, turning up her nose considerably:

"'Do you cats in the country eat fish?' and Mrs. Pussy replied:

"'Why, yes, of course we do; don't you?'

"'Certainly not; it is thought to be a sign of ill-breeding to eat such vulgar food,' and then remembering that she could not offer her cousin the least little thing, she said, never stopping to think very much about it, 'We eat mice here. They are delicious; you would be surprised to know what a delicate flavor they have.'

"That surprised the country cousin, and nothing would do but that she must go right out hunting for mice. Of course someone had to go with her, and then it was that the city cat found she hadn't made any such a very great mistake after all, for mice or rats, take them any way you please, cooked or raw, are very nice indeed."

A cat in distress,
Nothing more, nor less;
Good Folks, I must faithfully tell ye,
As I am a sinner,
It waits for some dinner
To stuff out its own little belly.

Percy Bysshe Shelley

Cats know how to obtain
food without labor, shelter without
confinement, and love without penalties.

W.L. GEORGE

In the blithe days of honeymoon,
With Kate's allurements smitten,
I lov'd her late, I lov'd her soon,
And call'd her dearest kitten.

But now my kitten's grown a cat,
And cross like other wives,
O! by my soul, my honest Mat,
I fear she has nine lives.

James Boswell

In a cat's eye,
all things belong to cats.

{ English proverb }

I came home from work one night and found our large, orange tabby sound asleep in the silverware drawer. Earlier that day, my husband, Mark, had left the drawer slightly ajar, and for some cat reason, Peaches decided that was where he wanted to sleep. He has claimed more than a dozen places in the house, but always has to check out whatever is a little different. We were amazed that Peaches fit through the drawer opening and could lay out flat enough to be in the drawer.

Mark got worried about Peaches being able to breathe and decided to pull him out, but the cat was wedged in so tightly, the drawer wouldn't open! After much effort, Mark finally got Peaches out of the drawer.

Peaches lay in his arms like a baby, shook his head a bit, and opened his eyes halfway, as if wondering what the commotion was all about.

Becky B.

TOP TEN

Things to Do While on a Bird Stakeout

- ✦ Practice exotic bird calls
- ✦ Take a catnap, of course
- ✦ Use binoculars to check out the neighbor's pet parakeet
- ✦ Text friends to ask for good barbeque bird recipes
- ✦ File nails to a fine point
- ✦ Cross-stitch a pillowcase for a feather pillow
- ✦ Watch humans with night-vision goggles
- ✦ Practice intimidating poses and flexes
- ✦ Decide which human to present the bird to and write a card
- ✦ Ponder deep life questions like: What is the victory of a cat on a hot tin roof?

I have lost many an hour of much-needed **sleep** from my cat's habit of coming upstairs at four A.M. and jumping suddenly upon the bed; perhaps landing on the pit of my stomach. Waking in that fashion, unsympathetic persons would have pardoned me if I had indulged in injudicious language, or had even thrown the cat violently from my otherwise peaceful couch. But conscience has not to upbraid me with any of these things. I flatter myself that I bear even this **patiently**; I remember to have often made sleepy but pleasant remarks to the faithful little friend whose affection for me and whose desire to behold my countenance was too great to permit her to **wait** till breakfast time.

Helen Winslow, from *Concerning Cats*

Going on a camping trip usually didn't include our large spoiled cat. But at the last minute, our neighbor said she couldn't watch Fluffy. Our three young daughters begged us to take our pet, so we packed an old dog leash and insisted Fluffy be watched at all times.

Everything went fine until it came time to break camp.

"Where's Fluffy?" I asked.

No one knew. Apparently Fluffy had gone exploring. We searched all over, but soon it was time to leave. We left our contact information with every camper in the remote lake area, and with many tears, we headed home.

* * *

During the next weekend, my brother Tom and his friends went camping.

After a long day of fishing, the exhausted teens crawled into their sleeping bags. In the middle of the night, Tom let out a scream, scrambled out of his bag, and yelled that something furry was crawling on him!

When everyone settled down, my brother realized the furry animal was a cat...a very familiar cat. *It can't be!* he thought. *How could ole Fluff get up here?* Because the cat was friendly, Tom fed her and kept her around. When the weekend was over, Tom took the cat and headed home.

He called me to relate his incredible story about a cat that was just like ours.

Fluffy was found!

When Tom brought her to our house the next weekend, we had a joyous reunion. We still laugh when we picture Fluffy's joy at finding a family member and Tom's sudden shock at waking to a furry critter nuzzling his cheek and pawing his face.

● Donna J.

A charm of cats is that
they seem to live in
a world of their own,
just as much as if it were
a real dimension of space.

Harriet Prescott Spofford

They say the test of literary power is
whether a man can write an inscription.
I say, "Can he name a kitten?"

SAMUEL BUTLER 🐾

Sid was a mellow cat. He never got excited about much and always moved at a leisurely pace. One time I noticed that he didn't seem to be up-to-par. It wasn't something my non-cat-person husband, Tom, could see, so I tried to explain that Sid seemed lethargic lately. My husband's response was, "How can you tell?"

After about a week of voicing my concern over what I perceived to be Sid's lack of responsiveness to food or affection, my long-suffering husband decided to take the cat to a vet while I was away at a retreat.

When I returned, Tom informed me that the cat had yowled all the way to the doctor's office and then prowled around the examination room, meowing plaintively. My husband ended up paying fifty dollars to learn that "there's nothing wrong with this cat."

From then on, Tom often pointed to a lounging Sid and exclaimed, "Look, honey! I think he's lethargic!"

Mrs. Dickerson

"**Praskovya,** there's a mouse caught! Bring the kitten here!"

"I'm coming," responded Praskovya, and a minute later she came in with the descendant of tigers in her arms.

"Capital!" said Pyotr Demyanitch, rubbing his hands. "We will give him a lesson. Put him down opposite the mouse-trap. That's it... Let him sniff it and look at it. That's it."

The kitten looked wonderingly at my uncle, at his arm-chair, sniffed the mouse-trap in bewilderment, then, frightened probably by the glaring lamplight and the attention directed to him, made a dash and ran in terror to the door.

"Stop!" shouted my uncle, seizing him by the tail. "Stop, you rascal! He's afraid of a mouse, the idiot! Look! It's a mouse! Look! Well? Look, I tell you!"

Anton Chekhov, from *Who Was to Blame?*

Cats find malicious amusement in doing what they are not wanted to do, and that with an affectation of innocence that materially aggravates their deliberate offense.

Helen Winslow

I am as vigilant as a cat
to steal cream.

{ William Shakespeare }

A friend related to me that they had a **cat** in her father's family who was a great favorite, and who was particularly fond of **the baby**; that one day this child was very fretful, and sat for a long time on the floor crying, and that nothing would pacify her.

The cat was by her side on the floor, and finding herself not noticed, and perhaps wearied at the noise, she suddenly stood up on her hind legs and **boxed** the child's ears in exactly the same way in which she was in the habit of boxing her **kitten's**.

Mrs. Eliza Lee Follen, from *True Stories About Cats and Dogs*

BEWARE OF CAT

TOP TEN

Songs Cats Love

+ "The Trout Quintet" by Franz Schubert
+ "Stray Cat Strut" by The Stray Cats
+ "Snowbird" by Anne Murray
+ "Cat's in the Cradle" by Harry Chapin
+ "I Want to Be Evil" by Eartha Kitt
+ "What's New Pussycat?" by Tom Jones
+ "Josie and the Pussycats" by Juliana Hatfield and Tanya Donelly
+ *Finding Nemo* (movie soundtrack) by Thomas Newman
+ any song by The Byrds
+ *Songs of the Cat* CD by Garrison Keillor and opera star Frederica Von Stade
  **Bonus track every cat loves: "Fish Heads" by Barnes and Barnes

One weekend I "cat-sat" for my lovely cat-niece, Ramona. While my sister was away, I posed Ramona and took pictures of her walking on the mantel, standing on the table amid empty cheese and meat containers, and drinking from bottles. For the final photo, I held up a teacup and encouraged Ramona to stand up on her hind legs to reach for it. With my hand out of the frame, I snapped the picture. To this day, my sister must secretly wonder if Ramona really *can* juggle china.

PERSONAL DISCLAIMER: I'm sure I didn't stage anything that Ramona herself hasn't done when left alone! Have you counted your teacups lately?

©Hope L.

Three friends and I were practicing a song for Easter Sunday. After running through the song a few times, Naomi said, "It's too bad we don't have someone to listen to us."

I called, "Kalli!"

My calico cat soon appeared from a back bedroom. She came into the living room where we were and sat down in front of us. She gave us a look that said, "Well?"

We all laughed and then started singing. We went through all five verses of the song while Kalli patiently and intently looked at us. When we were done, she stayed a few more seconds and then stood up and went back to the bedroom.

She never did tell us whether she liked the song, but since she didn't howl or hiss, we figured she did. My friends were quite impressed by my cat . . . and so was I!

@Barb G.

My husband claims he's indifferent to cats—but actions speak louder than words. He's been buying feathered lures for five dollars a pop. The feathers attach to a rod and string, and zip through the air like live birds. The cats destroy the feathers, so the toy goes on a tall bookcase during the day.

The minute Theo and Luna hear Don's car pull in, they run and perch on his armchair. Here's the routine: Back door opens; man enters; cats look winsome and neglected; man says accusingly, "Hasn't anyone played with the cats today?" and sighs; man goes to the bookcase like it's a chore akin to garbage hauling; man and cats play for ten minutes and everyone is happy.

Theo has learned to jump and get the lure down for Luna, but they don't really enjoy the game without Dad.

Dawn C.

Our cat always scratches at the front door until we open it. He marches directly from the door to the food dish, eats a little, and walks back to the front door.

One time I let him out and called, "Thank you for patronizing our establishment." My husband got such a kick out of that phrase that it has become a regular part of the exit routine.

PEGGY D. 🐾

The race of **cats**, it is true, has got a bad name, because we do not choose, like the dog, tamely to put up with all that men do to us. We hate slavery, and preserve our independence; and, opposed to all oppression, we do not show forth our talents at command.

Puss, from *Puss in Boots* by Charles Perrault

A cat's got her own opinion of human beings. She don't say much, but you can tell enough to make you anxious not to hear the whole of it.

JEROME K. JEROME

The cat went here and there
And the moon spun round like a top,
And the nearest kin of the moon,
The creeping cat, looked up.
Black Minnaloushe stared at the moon,
For, wander and wail as he would,
The pure cold light in the sky
Troubled his animal blood.
Minnaloushe runs in the grass
Lifting his delicate feet,
Do you dance, Minnaloushe,
do you dance?

WILLIAM BUTLER YEATS 🐾

The cat keeps his side of the bargain... He will kill
mice, and he will be kind to babies when he is in the
house, just so long as they do not pull his tail too
hard. But when he has done that, and between times,
and when the moon gets up and night comes, he is
the Cat that walks by himself, and all places are alike
to him. Then he goes out to the Wet Wild Woods or
up on the Wet Wild Trees or on the Wet Wild Roofs,
waving his wild tail and walking by his wild lone.

Rudyard Kipling

A cat that takes your food and growls at you for the favor, a cat that would eat you if he dared, is a pretty revelation... My cats at San Lorenzo knew some few moments of peace between two and three in the afternoon. That would have been the time to get up a testimonial to the **kind soul** who fed them. Try them at five and they would ignore you. But try them next morning!

Maurice Hewlett, from *Cats*

God made the cat in order that man might have the **pleasure** of caressing the tiger.

Fernand Mery

One of the most striking differences between a cat and a lie is that a cat has only nine lives.

Mark Twain

Cats do not have to be shown how to have a good time, for they are unfailing ingenious in that respect.

James Mason

The last thing I would
accuse a cat of is innocence.

{ Edward Paley }

I have noticed that what cats most appreciate in a human being is not the ability to produce food which they take for granted— but his or her entertainment value.

Geoffrey Household

Cat: A pygmy lion who loves mice, hates dogs, and patronizes human beings.

OLIVER HERFORD 🐾

TOP TEN

Things on a Cat's Bucket List

+ Invent canned mouse and make millions
+ Visit the Sahara—Hello…a free for all!
+ Bite a mail carrier
+ Master a pressurized whipped cream canister
+ Write a Broadway hit musical called *Humans*
+ Do stand-up comedy
+ Get over the fear of rocking chairs
+ Watch *Old Yeller* in a stadium-seating movie theater
+ Travel to the moon (it's made of cheese, you know)
+ Star in a remake of *Tom and Jerry* in which Tom gets Jerry!

Cats **love** one so much—
more than they will allow.
But they have so much wisdom
they keep it to themselves.

Mary E. Wilkins Freeman

The cat always leaves a mark on his friend.

AESOP 🐾

I had a regular bedroom at the bottom of a cup-board, with a feather pillow and triple-folded rug. The food was as good as the bed; no bread or soup, nothing but meat, good under-done meat.

Well! amidst all these comforts, I had but one wish, but one dream, to slip out by the half-open window, and run away on to the tiles. Caresses appeared to me insipid, the softness of my bed disgusted me, I was so fat that I felt sick, and from morn till eve I experienced the weariness of being happy.

Emilé Zola

"But I don't want to go among mad people," Alice remarked.

"Oh, you can't help that," said the Cat, "we're all mad here. I'm mad. You're mad."

"How do you know I'm mad?" said Alice.

"You must be," said the Cat, "or you wouldn't have come here."

Alice didn't think that proved it at all; however, she went on, "And how do you know that you're mad?"

"To begin with," said the Cat, "a dog's not mad. You grant that?"

"I suppose so," said Alice.

"Well, then," the Cat went on, "you see, a dog growls when it's angry, and wags its tail when it's pleased. Now I growl when I'm pleased, and wag my tail when I'm angry. Therefore I'm mad."

©Lewis Carroll, from *The Cheshire Cat*

For I will consider my Cat Jeoffry...
  For having done duty and received blessing
  he begins to consider himself.
For this he performs in ten degrees.
For first he looks upon his forepaws to see
    if they are clean.
For secondly he kicks up behind to clear away there.
For thirdly he works it upon stretch with the
    forepaws extended.
For fourthly he sharpens his paws by wood.
For fifthly he washes himself.
For sixthly he rolls upon wash.
For seventhly he fleas himself, that he may
    not be interrupted upon the beat.
For eighthly he rubs himself against a post.
For ninthly he looks up for his instructions.
For tenthly he goes in quest of food.

Christopher Smart, from *Rejoice in the Lamb*

Cats are a mysterious kind of folk. There is more passing in their minds than we are aware of.

Sir Walter Scott

There is no more intrepid explorer than a kitten.

{ Jules Champfleury }

As time went on, and they grew to know each other better, she began to find the kitchen cat a far superior companion to either her dolls or the man in the picture. True, it could not answer her any more than they did—in words, but it had a language of its own which she understood perfectly. She knew when it was pleased, and when it said "Thank you" for some delicacy she brought for it; its yellow eyes beamed with sympathy and interest when she described the delights of that beautiful life it would enjoy in the nursery; and when she pitied it for the darkness of its present dwelling below, she knew it understood by the way it rubbed against her and arched up its back. There were many more pleasures in each day now that she had made this acquaintance.

Amy Walton, from *The Kitchen Cat*

Puss jumped upon the great arm-chair. Theophilus explained to the shoemaker that he was required to take his young friend's measure for a pair of boots. The man, although a little astonished, was very glad to get a fresh job; he concealed the slight alarm which he felt; and even when Puss leaned one paw upon his head, he only requested the young gentleman to draw in his claws a little. In taking the measure, the shoemaker stroked Puss's leg, which set him purring with pleasure, and he addressed his master, "Good Theophilus, I love you; you never stroked me the wrong way; you let me sleep quietly in the sun; and when your brothers wanted to tease me, and carried me into the dark, in order to see what they called electrical sparks from my back, you always opposed it: I will now show my gratitude for all this."

Charles Perrault, from *Puss in Boots*

If animals could speak,
the dog would be a blundering outspoken fellow,
but the cat would have the rare grace
of never saying a word too much.

{ Mark Twain }